Overcoming Moral Failure

Picking Up the Pieces

GORDON S. FROESE

CROSSBOOKS
PUBLISHING

CrossBooks™
A Division of LifeWay
1663 Liberty Drive
Bloomington, IN 47403
www.crossbooks.com
Phone: 1-866-879-0502

Scriptures taken from the Holy Bible, New International Version®, NIV®.
Copyright © 1973, 1978, 1984, 2011 by Biblica, Inc.™ Used by permission
of Zondervan. All rights reserved worldwide. www.zondervan.com The
"NIV" and "New International Version" are trademarks registered in
the United States Patent and Trademark Office by Biblica, Inc.™

First published by CrossBooks 12/13/2013

ISBN: 978-1-4627-3291-3 (sc)
ISBN: 978-1-4627-3293-7 (hc)
ISBN: 978-1-4627-3292-0 (e)

Library of Congress Control Number: 2013919931

Printed in the United States of America.

This book is printed on acid-free paper.

Any people depicted in stock imagery provided by Thinkstock are models,
and such images are being used for illustrative purposes only.
Certain stock imagery © Thinkstock.

Contents

Foreword

FOR ABOUT THE PAST TWELVE years Gordon Froese has been part of my life; first as a fellow church attender, then as a dentist, and now, as a repentant seeker of healing and restoration. It has been my privilege to walk closely with him on this journey. Through weekly meetings and other activities I have watched and listened to his life. I and others have encouraged him to share his thoughts and experience.

Gordon writes out of a deep brokenness which he describes clearly and vividly. Tears are not necessarily proof of that brokenness, but many have flowed out of it. That brokenness started him on the road to restoration and continues to mark his life.

Repentance, a change of direction, came as he let his heart be crushed by the awfulness of his sin. It included a walk toward restoration with people he had hurt. He continues to travel with a repentant heart.

The pages of this book are marked with a brutal honesty. I have been an observer of it. That honesty is in his life, not just on the pages of this book. He came to the point where he stopped lying to himself and others. Authenticity marks him day by day.

These principles are clearly presented in these pages and are underscored with the teaching of the Bible. They are presented with a desire to help others recover from moral failure and move toward a life of integrity and positive influence. May this book be used in the lives of the many people who are presently living in moral failure.

Del McKenzie, retired pastor and friend

Introduction

MORAL FAILURE IS A PROBLEM that has plagued human beings since the beginning of time. All of life is filled with choices. Often those choices involve choosing between right and wrong. We all know of people who have chosen badly and have caused themselves and those they love much pain. There is a God who created us and gave us the Bible to help us to understand what he knows to be right and wrong. You will find as you read this book that he is an expert on moral failure, first because he defines right and wrong, and secondly because he has been watching men make fools of themselves through their bad judgment for thousands of years. He also has been seeking to help men and women to avoid moral failure, and when they do fail, he provides a way out of the mess. Every bad choice that we make is against the teaching of Scripture and offends the God who made us for his pleasure.

It is probably safe to assume that if you are reading this, you either know someone or you are someone who has become entrapped by moral failure. It is my intention to be direct and firm. It is just as much my intention to also lovingly give you hope that there is not only a way out but also a way back from a messed-up life to restoration. God is all about helping you to pick up the pieces of a broken life and producing in you a new, healthy, and happy life. "God demonstrates his own love for us in this: "While we were still sinners, Christ died for us" (Romans 5:8). "The Lord is … patient with you, not wanting anyone to perish, but everyone to come to repentance" (2 Peter 3:9).

One of my favorite passages of Scripture is Jeremiah 18:1–4: "I went down to the potter's house, and I saw him working at the wheel. But the pot he was shaping from the clay was marred in his hands; so the potter formed it into another pot, shaping it as seemed best to him." Marred and broken pots are all that we are when we are enslaved by moral failure. My purpose in sharing the words on these pages is to show a process by which a marred pot can be formed into another pot, shaped as seems best to God. There is hope!

Some might ask what right I have to write about overcoming moral failure. They have every right to ask that question, and the answer is quite simple. I was involved in an adulterous affair for over ten years. During that time I fabricated every possible excuse, all the while longing for deliverance from the power of my sin. Frequently I would ask myself and God, "Why can't I get free from this awful thing?" It was slowly destroying me from the inside out! Scripture says, "The wages of sin is death." I was slowly dying. My physical health was failing, I was depressed, and my spirit was in constant conflict. To continue in moral failure of any kind will destroy you, as well as those with whom you are involved. The word "moral" means "having to do with right (vs. wrong) behavior or conduct." There are patterns of behavior that I have observed not only in myself but also in others. Guilt, denial, hopelessness, despair, and many other emotions flooded my soul that all reinforced the moral failure that needed to be overcome.

I am writing this because, after giving my testimony at a men's retreat, I met a fellow who thought there was no freedom from moral failure once you have tasted it. After more than eight years of freedom, I can say to you that stating that it is impossible to overcome moral failure is a flat-out lie of the Devil, the enemy of our souls. It is neither a foregone conclusion nor a necessity. With God's help, and with the help of other fellow human beings whom he employed, I was able to overcome my failure—and you can too! Please listen to my story and bear with me as I try to, with the help of God and his Word, the Bible, show you what happened and explain how you, too, can overcome your own moral failure and become, as it is said in Romans 8:37, "more than conquerors!"

I will make numerous references to the Bible. These Scriptures helped me to understand my own nature and the nature of moral failure in a way that is astoundingly accurate. This should not be surprising. If the one who created us is the same God who wrote the Bible, his observations on human behavior should be accurate. For me it only helped to prove that God did inspire the Holy Scriptures. "As for God, his way is perfect; the word of the Lord is flawless" (Psalm 18:30). "The law of the Lord is perfect, reviving the soul. The statutes of the Lord are trustworthy, making wise the simple" (Psalm 19:7).

Take Proverbs chapter 9, for example. Verses 1–6 give us hope that we can leave our errant ways. Wisdom says to "those who lack judgment ... to come and ... leave your simple ways." Who are those who lack judgment? "A man who commits adultery lacks judgment; whoever does so destroys himself" (Proverbs 6:32). Wow, what could be more accurate than that statement? My own young daughter confirmed this appraisal of adultery when I confessed to her that I had used poor judgment. She responded that I had not used poor judgment or even bad judgment, but no judgment at all! Wham! The next section of Proverbs 9 discusses the rebuking of a mocker, as opposed to a wise man, and that "the fear of the Lord is the beginning of wisdom." We can change if we will listen to sound advice. The last part of this proverb describes the woman, Folly, one who leaves God out of his or her thoughts. She invites those who "lack judgment" to come to her because "stolen water is sweet; food eaten in secret is delicious!" "But little do they know that the dead are there, that her guests are in the depths of the grave." Is there a more accurate description of the process of moral failure?

Adultery is not the only way a person can commit moral failure. It is just one of many methods. Galatians 5:19–21 puts it this way:

"The acts of the sinful nature are obvious: sexual immorality, impurity and debauchery: idolatry and witchcraft; hatred, dissensions, factions and envy; drunkenness, orgies and the like." In 1 John 3:4, we read, "Sin is lawlessness." And in 1 John 5:17, "All wrong doing is sin." In simplicity, any behavior that goes against a code of ethics, whether man's or God's, and as a result requires one to hide it or to use deceit of any kind to keep it from the eyes of others or from God is moral failure.

If you are caught in some trap and are looking for help, then I hope and pray that what I share here will be useful to you in finding the road back from moral failure and overcoming that failure to the point of complete deliverance.

This is from one fellow ragamuffin to another ragamuffin.

Please read Brennan Manning's book *Ragamuffin Gospel*.

Chapter 1

The Anatomy of Moral Failure

To BEGIN WE MUST HAVE an understanding of what moral failure is and how it happens. While there are many examples of moral failure, none is more helpful than that of the story of Achan in the Bible in Joshua, chapter 7.

The context is the Israelites' siege of Jericho. In Joshua 6:17–19, the whole city of Jericho was to be devoted to Jehovah, especially the precious metals and other articles of value. This means they were to be placed in the treasury of the Lord. Achan violated this edict, disobeying the command of God. Moral failure often involves taking or appropriating for ourselves that which does not belong to us.

His confession is particularly enlightening. In Joshua 7:19–21 Achan says, "Indeed I have sinned against the Lord God of Israel, and thus and thus have I done: when I saw among the spoils a goodly Babylonish garment, and two hundred shekels of silver, and a wedge of gold of fifty shekels weight, then I coveted them, and took them, and, behold they are hid in the earth in the midst of my tent, and the silver under it."

Let's take a closer look at Achan's confession. First he says, "I have sinned against the Lord God of Israel." He admitted, and we must also admit, that sinning is against the Lord God. When King David sinned by committing adultery, he said "Against thee, thee (God) only have I sinned and done this evil in thy sight" (Psalm 51:4). We might ask if he didn't sin against the woman, her husband, and his own wife as well as God. Well, yes. But when I sin against anyone, God takes it personally; therefore, my sin ultimately is the activity of my will against the will of God. While the effect of a sin is felt by those around us, sin is against God.

Yes, Achan had sinned, but besides admitting that he had sinned against the Lord God of Israel, Achan confessed to how he sinned. He specifically used four verbs that are very instructive: "saw," "coveted," "took," and "hid." Commit these to memory! When moral failure occurs, it almost always falls upon these lines and in that order.

Achan first *looked* and *saw* something attractive. Even though God had expressly forbidden taking these things, Achan looked at them long enough to consider what advantage they might provide for him. Then he went from just looking and contemplating or appreciating them to *coveting* them. He wanted them, in spite of God's command and the fact that they were not his to take. The next step was *taking* them. He took for himself that which belonged to God. It naturally follows that once we disobey, stealing from God or others, taking what does not belong to us or even behaving in a way that is disobedient to God's will, then we have to *hide* the stuff, the act, the misbehavior, or the moral failure to avoid exposure and conviction.

This is very similar to the original sin of Adam and Eve. They *saw* that the fruit of the tree, the one tree God had forbidden them to eat from, was good for food, pleasant to the eyes, and a tree to be desired (*coveted*) to make one wise. Then Eve *took* the fruit and ate and shared with Adam, who also ate. They were guilty of disobedience. They realized they were naked and began sewing fig leaves together to clothe themselves in order to *hide* that nakedness. This was the first religious effort of humans to try to become acceptable to God. I see the definition of "religion" as "any human-devised effort to make ourselves acceptable to God." When they heard God probing and looking for them, Adam's response was, "I was afraid because I was naked, and I *hid* myself." Wow, same pattern!

All behavior that is ungodly or morally wrong is summarized in the Bible in 1 John 2:16–17: "For everything in the world—the cravings of sinful man, the lust of his eyes and the boasting of what he has and does—comes not from the Father but from the world. The world and its desires pass away, but the man who does the will of God lives forever." It is interesting how these three things are so evident in the transgressions of Adam and Eve and of Achan.

are follows the same pattern of these prototypes. God

ning and sees everything, so why do we think we can

never surprise God. His Word makes it abundantly clear that he understands our behavior and wants to provide us with a means of deliverance from the bondage of moral failure. In order to get to the point of deliverance, we must understand the anatomy of moral failure. It is critically necessary for us to understand how we got into the mess we are in before we can find the way out of it. Therefore, it is necessary to expand a little on each of the four aspects of moral failure. Each of these aspects may take only a brief moment of time, or even years, to grow and become fully mature. Time is not a factor, but the longer it takes to develop, the deeper the roots of slavery to moral failure become.

We *look* at, contemplate, and dream about the cravings of sinful man (carnal lust), the lust of the eyes, and the boasting of what we have or do instead of turning away from what is not rightfully ours.

We *covet*, desire, and then begin to lie to ourselves about how things we don't need would be good or beneficial or so much better than what we have now. We tell ourselves that it is okay to covet because we deserve better than what we have now. We tell ourselves that we will miss out on some wonderful opportunity, or that we need things to cope with a horrible situation. Really, the lies we tell ourselves are endless and as numerous as the number of people lying.

Then we come to the point of *taking* it, plunging in and grasping whatever it is that has gotten our attention. As I said before, this may happen slowly by degrees or quickly, depending on the tenderness or hardness of our conscience. It may happen slowly as we vacillate back and forth between looking and coveting, maybe taking just a taste or a little bit here and there until we are eventually brought under the power of whatever it is we succumb to.

The last step is coming to the point of realizing that our actions are not acceptable. Now we have a problem! That fact alone should cause us to give up and turn away from our poor option. But depending on how much time and energy we have given to looking, coveting, and taking, it may not be possible to alter our course. It then becomes necessary to *hide* what we are doing from others. Lying becomes a necessity, first to continue lying to ourselves and then to prevent others from discovering what we've done. I call it a necessity because if we don't hide, then we become accountable and may be forced to relinquish our newly acquired treasure. We become very skilled at deceit. The longer we practice our moral failure and consequent deceit, the better we get at it. We create smoke screens and excuses, often by doing good activities, especially anything that casts us in a better light. Sometimes we might even engage in good behavior, hoping that somehow the good behavior might help deliver us from the trap into which we have fallen. In this case, three purposes are served. First, we believe that by lying to ourselves, we may be able to convince ourselves that we aren't that bad. Second, we tell ourselves that if we do enough good, it will somehow either outweigh our failures or even refocus our activities or efforts and become a means of deliverance. Thirdly, we satisfy ourselves that good actions will help deceive others, making them think we are good guys who would never stray from the straight-and-narrow way.

In summary, moral failure happens when we look at some forbidden object, relationship, substance, goal, or temptation of any sort long enough and with enough intensity that we begin to covet it. This coveting drives us to the point of taking it, grasping it, or maybe just sampling it until it gets a hold of us and we do not want to relinquish it. This in turn requires us to begin lying to ourselves and hiding our actions from others. The others are those who are especially close to us. We hide from them in order to continue on our wrong paths with some semblance of normal goodness. After all, no one wants to look bad.

Chapter 2

Costs and Effects of Moral Failure

IT IS AN UNDERSTATEMENT TO say that there are many consequences that follow moral failure. The longer we persist on the path of moral failure, the more those complications become compounded. While I will discuss some of these, the list is unlimited. If you are reading this and have been, or know, a participant in moral failure, you could add to this discussion significantly. You will doubtless be able to identify with the various points that I can recall or that I've observed in others. My hope is that you will recognize that experiencing moral failure is the equivalent of being a fool in the extreme. "A man who commits adultery lacks judgment; whoever does so destroys himself" (Proverbs 6:32). Note that this verse refers not to poor judgment or bad judgment, but to the *absence* of judgment or discernment! This verse summarizes the whole discussion of the effects and consequences of moral failure—the destruction of the perpetrator and damage to all those attached to him or her. Proverbs 5–7 describes in detail the moral failure that is, perhaps, the most obvious, and also that which I was guilty of:

adultery. However, any moral failure you can imagine can easily be substituted for adultery in this passage. Who or what is your mistress?

Let's look first at the personal costs of moral failure. Yes, there is a huge price to be paid, and not just in dollars, though that is a consideration as well. If each individual involved in moral failure weighed the cost of their action before they ever took that first step, they would find it to be staggering, and perhaps this would spare them and their surrounding circle an incalculable amount of suffering. But we are such idiots that we do not even think in terms of what will be the real result of our instant gratification.

I found that moral failure required time. It took up time that could have been spent constructively, time that I could have spent with my family, time that I could have spent doing things that matter, time that I could have spent doing a better job. The list goes on and on. The immoral behavior you engage in not only takes time but also reduces your performance and productivity in the things that matter. That is time that is lost forever! The sin itself takes time, but I found that it also took even more time to cover my tracks, to explain (lie), to make excuses, etc. There will be more on that subject later, in chapter 3, "Necessary Evasive Tactics."

Some of the greatest personal costs in my experience with moral failure were internal, or emotional. That is, moral failure aroused my conscience, which in turn produced immense quantities of guilt, shame, and eventually, depression; it even caused my blood pressure to rise! This resulted in a drastic reduction in quality of life, though all the while I deceived myself into thinking that I was trying to improve my quality of life! What an irony! All of these things led to the severe straining of relationships, both close (family) and extended (at work, at church, with neighbors, etc.). Ultimately, if you persist, as I did, the result will be damage that is very difficult to repair and can easily, in some cases, be permanent. The cost of this pain to me, as well as the pain of guilt, shame, and sense of failure, was crippling to say the least.

The apostle Paul said, "'Everything is permissible for me.'- but I will not be mastered by anything … The body is not meant for sexual (or any other) immorality, but for the Lord, and the Lord for the body … Flee from sexual (or any other) immorality … he who sins sexually sins against his own body. Do you not know that your body is a temple of the Holy Spirit, who is in you, whom you have received from God? You are not your own; you were bought at a price. Therefore honor God with your body" (1 Corinthians 6:12–20).

As these emotions and stresses ate away at my soul, I began to shrivel inside. There was a decrease in my overall health, an increase in my blood pressure, and, among other things, a decrease in my energy. In fact, after a while I felt that I was slowly dying from the inside out.

> He who commits adultery … destroys himself.
> (Proverbs 6:32)

The wages of sin is death. (Romans 6:23)

The mind of sinful man is death. (Romans 8:6)

This is not what God wants; it is what God tells us will happen. It is the natural course of events when we engage in unhealthy behavior. These internal effects produced a great cost to my health emotionally, mentally, physically, and, even more important, spiritually.

But it does not end there. All this inner turmoil resulted in more personal damage. I lost my dignity and reduced my self-esteem and sense of self-worth and confidence. I felt that if I could not control this aspect of my life, I could not do much of anything right. I also made some other very poor decisions that reinforced my huge sense of being a failure, which indeed was exactly appropriate.

Another cost is the material cost. In order to satisfy our craving, whatever that craving may be, it may well cost us in dollars, the obtaining of the object of our craving, the maintenance of that object, and the hiding of it. We also run the risk of losing material possessions as a consequence of possessing things that are not rightly ours.

Loss of reputation is another astronomical cost. Who can measure the value of the reputation of a good name? The fear of losing one's reputation is one of the reasons we tell ourselves that we can't come clean and expose ourselves. We should weigh these costs before making the decision whether or not to go down the road of moral failure.

There were also less obvious effects and costs resulting from my moral failure, including the time and energy spent in trying to cover up and hide my behavior. In order to continue in bad behavior, we *must* cover up and hide it; otherwise, the curtain falls down and we are exposed. Then there is the time and energy spent in trying to escape from the bondage in which we find ourselves, and the regrets of feeling trapped. Indeed I was trapped. I have no idea how much I spent in time, energy, and emotional scheming, plotting, and attempting to escape from the trap that I had created for myself.

Next we must look at another cost that, for me, is much harder to assess and to discuss. In fact, this may be the hardest part of this book to write. We have confronted some of the costs to me personally, but perhaps the greater cost is the awful collateral damage to those close to me. We get into these kinds of circumstances for very selfish reasons. We do not take into account what the effect on our loved ones will be. The effect that my moral failure had on my family and those close to me was far more than I could estimate or even begin to describe to you. I am sure that I still do not have an accurate appraisal of the damage that I caused. To have my son walk out of the house and stay away from me for over a year, to have my daughters censure and shun me and listen to my wife weeping and abhorring the thought of me touching her—this is only the tip of the iceberg, and I deserved much worse.

The shame and humiliation suffered by my family, the effect on their reputations, and their pain upon finding out that their husband, father, son, brother, brother-in-law or uncle was living a lie were astounding. This was, for me, one of the greatest causes of shame and repentance. If only I could have considered this before. The consideration of the pain I had caused was one of the major factors in my repentance and turning away from my sin. I must confess that I have only a small comprehension of the damage I caused my loved ones. They are still in the process of healing and recovering, as am I. Besides the devastation, which was so great, their loss of ability to trust me was crushing both for them as well as for me. That loss of trust is fundamental to consider when it comes to rebuilding. That loss goes on costing for a long, long time! In some cases it never is rebuilt. Do you really want to cause those you love this much pain? If so, it is an abominable way to show love.

The total cost of moral failure is impossible to calculate, but I can tell you it is great and becomes greater the longer you engage in your bad behavior. Not only does the cost increase as time goes on, but the difficulty of escaping increases as well when we become more entrenched.

Chapter 3

Necessary Evasive Tactics

ONCE A PERSON BECOMES ENTRAPPED by his or her failure to maintain moral standards and wants to continue to embrace that failure, it becomes requisite that he or she become an expert in what I call necessary evasive tactics. I know this because I became an expert in it. Remember, in Adam and Eve's and Achan's sin, the fourth and last step in their moral failure was hiding. With Adam and Eve it was first fig leaves and then physically trying to hide from God—which, incidentally, you never can do. Achan tried burying his theft under his tent.

Adam and Eve were trying to make themselves acceptable by covering their nakedness, which is all that religion can do for us. Religion does not make us acceptable; it is just our attempt to make ourselves acceptable on our terms, not God's. Achan, on the other hand, tried to bury his sin under his domestic responsibility. I can identify with both of these tactics. I was teaching adult bible study and helping in the youth group in the church plus maintaining a busy dental practice, all of which take up lots of time and energy, but this gave me a screen of respectability behind which to hide. Because I was so busy with these activities, it was as though I was using them as alibis. This allowed me to withdraw from personal contacts and accountability. I became very skillful at avoidance and denial.

Fyodor Dostoevsky in *The Brothers Karamazov* had a friar say something very profound to one of his characters: "Stop lying, especially to yourself!" This has been like a sledgehammer to me, and it was one of the keys to ultimately setting me free. It must be understood that if anyone is going to continue in moral failure, lying and deceit will become a necessary way of life for that person. You can't do one without the other. I had to learn to act and become quite good at disguising the truth regarding my moral failure. What began as lies to myself escalated to the point of me being in denial of the wrongness of my behavior to the extent that I could justify to myself the lies and deceit that I foisted on those around me. I remember flat out denying direct questions from my good friend and pastor, as well as my dear wife, about my activities.

Evasive tactics involved other maneuvers for me, such as deflecting questions or misdirecting conversations that might be getting too close to the subject of my relationships. Changing the subject worked very well also. Offense is often the best defense, and so I frequently would employ that too. I would call this putting up a smoke screen. To give an example of this, I might comment on something from the Bible or even other moral ethics to give the appearance of spirituality and uprightness. I might also criticize someone else's moral failing. That is hypocrisy of the first degree! A friend of mine just called and said, "When I'm doing wrong, I am far more judgmental than when I am doing right!" How true that is.

There is a whole basketful of evasive tactics that can be used, such as manipulating people or circumstances to allow things to appear appropriate when they are not. The main ingredient in all of them, though, is deceit. Lying is necessary if you are engaged in anything that you do not want to be discovered. Just as zebras have stripes and leopards have spots, so anyone engaged in bad behavior or moral failure of any kind is a liar and deceiver. If you find that you can't be truthful about something, then you might well evaluate whether or not that activity or thing is morally right. And by the same token, if someone is not being truthful to you, that person may well be hiding something that is inappropriate.

Chapter 4

Point of Decision

S O, MY DEAR FRIEND, WHAT about you? Does any of this resonate with you? Does it ring any bells in your mind or heart? Have you messed up a little or a lot? If you have messed up, then you are in good company. Sound crazy? Some of God's best friends messed up big-time. Adam, Abraham, Jacob, Moses, Rahab, Gideon, Barak, Samson, Jephthah, David, Peter, Saul of Tarsus, and others are biblical figures whose flaws as human beings God saw fit to show us. So, again, I ask, "What about you?"

If you have messed up, then you have three choices:

1. Continue with slavery to your vice.
2. Fight it by yourself.
3. Confess, repent, and expose yourself to yourself and to others and get help.

With either of the first two choices, you will fail! If you are like me, then you will waste valuable time vacillating back and forth between the first two options. With the last choice, there is hope and victory, but only if you want it badly enough to "do whatever it takes," which will be hard and agonizing work. If you do chose to confess and expose yourself voluntarily, it is far more honorable than if you wait to be exposed involuntarily. If you do wait till you are involuntarily exposed, then the pathway back will be even more difficult, if such a thing can be. I was exposed involuntarily.

If you can honestly say, "I am willing to do whatever it takes," which is my personal mantra, then there is hope for you. There is victory in the end for those who persist in spite of difficulties. If you agree with this third option and want to be free, then I pray that you will continue to turn the pages of this book until you, too, find the map that shows you the way out of your personal prison. There will be a lot of big pills to swallow, but wouldn't it be great to be free? It is often said that freedom comes with a price. The choice is yours to pay the price of freedom or pay the price of continuing on in your slavery. In the long run, the price of freedom is far less than the price of bondage, because with freedom there is an end, but with bondage it just goes on and on.

Chapter 5

Excuses

I KNOW, I KNOW; YOU have a lot of excuses. I did. One of my dear pastor friends said, "You are just not thinking rightly!" Romans 2:15 says, "Their consciences also bearing witness, and their thoughts now accusing, now even defending [or excusing] them." When you are enslaved to moral failure, you have a conscience that will make you miserable by accusation or by making up excuses so that you can continue in your bad behavior and make yourself even more miserable.

Let's look at some of those many excuses. There is a common thread in all of these excuses, and it is the theme of selfishness.

"I like it—the feel, the taste, the rush, the sound, the power. It gives me pleasure." Sure, you like it for whatever reason because it pleases you now. That is called self-gratification. Scripture even acknowledges that there is pleasure in sin for a season. Does liking it or enjoying it make it right?

"I can't resist _____." Of course you can't. You can't resist anything if you don't *really* want to change. You may say you want to change, but you have not come to the end of yourself. Coming to the end of yourself is giving up your perceived rights to self-indulgence. It is hitting rock bottom, and you have not hit rock bottom if you think you can't resist. You will never change until the pain of your slavery becomes great enough.

"I have already done it once, so what's one more time?" One more time only helps to establish a pattern and to reinforce the bondage of your slavery, and the more times you reinforce it, the greater the bondage.

"I could not bear the exposure!" Four times in the gospels it is said that "nothing is covered, that shall not be revealed; and hid that shall not be known." You must know that eventually you will be exposed. You only have so much time to live. Are you going to live it out in slavery and be exposed when there is no time to repent? Or will you risk exposure and go through the pain that exposure carries with it and finally be able to begin to rebuild your life by repentance and confession so that you might spend the rest of your life in true freedom? John 8:32 says, "The truth shall make you free." In reality, it was a relief for me after the pain of exposure to finally have the truth be known and not have to hide anymore.

"Exposure would hurt my loved ones." That one is not as considerate as it sounds. Whether there is exposure or not, continuing in bad behavior hurts loved ones far more than exposure and healing. Have you ever considered how much your behavior is hurting them now? Yes, exposure hurts all those affected, but just as in surgery, until the damaged area is exposed and dealt with, the healing process can't begin.

"I really just don't want to quit." At least this one is possibly honest. If it is truly honest, then there is not much hope. But if this is bravado and underneath you do want to quit, then you need to keep reading. Selfishness is defined as being devoted to, or caring only for, oneself. Another word for this is "narcissism," which is defined as "inordinate self-love." Why would you not want to quit? This is a question you must face. Would it take too much effort, cost too much? Or is it that you simply enjoy the disobedience in which you are involved so much that you will not, or cannot, consider any other alternative? The word for this is "addiction," which is defined as "the state of being enslaved to a habit or practice or to something that is psychologically or physically habit forming." I would add to this any inappropriate or unhealthy relationship between individuals, or even a cause. If such is the case, then this is very revealing in respect to your perverted values. But then, all sin is the result of perverted values. What you want is more important to you than anything or anyone else. You are just plain selfish, and that is all that matters to you, regardless of how it affects others.

"It keeps me going." Part of this excuse is the result of that same selfishness again, while part of it is the result of being so invested in your moral failure that you think your life is deficient without engaging in your bad behavior. In other words, "I can't live without _____!" Again it just comes back to meeting your needs regardless of the effect on others.

This next excuse is one I employed repeatedly. "Once a _____, always a _____." This goes back to wrong thinking and lying to yourself. The conclusion of this line of faulty thinking is, "So why quit now?" How convenient! The fact is that "all of us have sinned and fall short of the glory of God" (Romans 3:23). Does this excuse mean that Jesus Christ did not come into the world to save sinners, but just to collect the "good" people around him? Quite the opposite! God is all about constantly inviting us to repent and turn to him; to convert—that is, to turn around and go the other way. To embrace this excuse directly denies that God has the ability to perform a change in us. What about the woman in John chapter 8 who was caught in adultery? Jesus told her accusers, "If any of you is without sin, let him be the first to throw a stone at her." After they all went away, did he say to her, "Sorry, woman, you are an adulteress and always will be and that is that, end of story!"? No! Instead, Jesus said to her, "Woman, where are they? Has no one condemned you?" She said, "No one, sir." "Then neither do I condemn you," Jesus declared. "Go now and leave your life of sin." He offered to her both forgiveness and the opportunity to not be what she was in the past. We can be changed!

Another related excuse is "I can't change; I can't overcome" or "I can never be free." If you read the introduction to this book, you might remember that this is one of the reasons I am writing. In Proverbs 9:4–6, wisdom invites us to do just that. "Let all who are simple come in here!" she (wisdom) says to those who lack judgment (he who commits adultery lacks judgment). "Come … Leave your simple ways and you will live; walk in the way of understanding." The only time I could not change was when I was simply not willing to do whatever it took to change.

Remember, you will never change until the pain of your slavery becomes great enough. Feeling the pain caused by my bad behavior was one of the most significant factors in moving me to the place of being willing to do whatever it took to change and begin to repair the damage. Saying that you can't change is just a cop-out, just another way of saying "I won't change" or "I don't want to change." The fact is that you can change if you want to badly enough. You just have to be willing to do whatever it takes. Do not weigh the consequences, because if you do you will lie to yourself and convince yourself that the risks are too great. That is fantasy. In reality the risks are too great not to change, and the rewards for doing whatever it takes are immeasurable.

Think long and hard about the pain you are enduring and the pain that you are inflicting on those around you. Think also about the tremendous cost of continuing in your behavior. If I had not repented but persisted in my course of destruction, I would have lost my children (which I did for a time anyway), my wife, my reputation, my friends, my extended family, everything familiar to me, and more than half my worldly worth. Repentance is simply reversing direction, with a permanent mindset, because of the realization of one's bad behavior and consequent destination.

Another excuse I employed was to assume that God had allowed my circumstances in order to permit my adulterous relationship to develop. This is blasphemy, as God in no way condones sin of any nature. There were times that I imagined it almost seemed as though I were being protected from detection and provided with opportunity by some divine intervention. That is blind and stupid audacity, and if that is not crazy thinking, I don't know what is! God will *never* assist anyone in a pathway of sinning against him. He will never be party to disobedience to his will.

What he will do is allow us to get so far down that we come to the end of ourselves, abhorring ourselves and our behavior, so that we will be willing to turn from our sin, rejecting it, and turn toward him for redemption. Redemption means "to buy back and to set at liberty (opposite of slavery)," and it always involves a cost. Yes, God has given us free will, and we can choose to obey him or to disobey him, though choosing to disobey him leads us to become enslaved to whatever bad behavior we have chosen. That almost always involves either saying no to our natural desires in order to obey him, or giving in to our natural desires in order to disobey him. I say "almost always" because not all of our natural desires are against his will; in fact, many are ordained by God. But if we persist in following our natural inclinations, we will soon be on a path that leads to sorrow and trouble.

Then there is the excuse of blaming others (besides God, which we have just discussed). "If only someone would be different (in any multitude of ways), then I could be different, and then I would not do what I am doing." It is amazing how many times that other someone is one's spouse. Another variation is "Someone just pushes me toward _____." Blame is simply a tool to relieve one of one's own responsibility. Politicians are especially good at this, but so are self-indulgent, morally failing human beings of any kind.

As was mentioned previously, we have been given free will and hence are constantly making choices that, when they turn out to have good results, we are quite ready to take responsibility for; but when the result is bad, hurtful, or just plain wrong, we are just as ready to shift the blame of that choice onto someone or something else. That blame could be cast on a person or a present or past circumstance.

What I needed to do was face my sin and take full responsibility for my behavior, my bad choices, and not just poor judgment, but bad judgment or lack of judgment. You can never get free until you are willing to look honestly at yourself in the mirror and acknowledge the responsibility that you have in becoming the monster that you have become. You can't blame anyone or anything else.

All excuses come down to wrong thinking. I was thinking wrongly when I was making excuses to continue on the wrong course I had embraced. We can't think rightly until we can be completely honest, first with ourselves and second with others—especially those we have hurt and those to whom we will be accountable. "Accountable" is a tough word for the morally depraved. Wrong thinking is a crutch for all of our excuses and enables us to justify our bad behavior to ourselves in order to continue on our chosen pathway of misbehavior. It is our means of coping with guilt and avoiding self-judgment and condemnation.

Chapter 6

Choice

So, MY DEAR FRIEND, HAVE you messed up? Have you crossed a line by choosing or giving in to a behavior that is against God and those around you, as well as harmful to you? Are you enslaved to something to which you have yielded and to which you are now in bondage?

In the daily devotional book *My Utmost for His Highest*, Oswald Chambers has a commentary entitled "Obedience" that focuses on the following passage in Romans 6:16: "His servants ye are to whom ye obey." Part of that commentary follows:

> The first thing to do in examining the power that dominates me is to take hold of the unwelcome fact that I am responsible for being thus dominated. If I am a slave to myself, I am to blame because at a point a way back I yielded to myself. Likewise, if I obey God I do so because I have yielded myself to Him.

Yield in childhood to selfishness, and you will find it the most enchaining tyranny on earth. There is no power in the human soul of itself to break the bondage of a disposition formed by yielding. Yield for one second to anything in the nature of lust (remember what lust is: 'I must have it at once,' whether it be the lust of the flesh or the lust of the mind) – once yield and though you may hate yourself for having yielded, you are a bond slave to that thing. There is no release in human power at all but only in the Redemption. You must yield yourself in utter humiliation to the only One Who can break the dominating power, viz., the Lord Jesus Christ – 'He hath anointed me … to preach deliverance to all captives.'

You find this out in the most ridiculously small ways –'Oh, I can give that habit up when I like.' You cannot, you will find that the habit absolutely dominates you because you yielded to it willingly. It is easy to sing – 'He will break every fetter' and at the same time be living a life of obvious slavery to yourself. Yielding to Jesus will break every form of slavery in any human life.

If you have chosen wrongly or yielded to something, or some behavior, then you are daily being faced with another choice. It is a choice, because when we sin, it is an action of exercising our will against God and man. Not choosing to do what is right is choosing to do wrong. It is not a slip, as in an accident. We decide to participate. Once we have entered on a pathway of sin, we are left with essentially four choices.

The first choice is the choice to continue to sin. In this situation, you just keep on a downward spiral toward calamity. This will lead to all kinds of guilt, frustration, depression, and possibly outright physical illness. Eventually your heart will harden, the guilt will decrease, and eventually you will care less and less about being in the wrong. You will become stuck in a rut and fail to overcome.

As a second option, you could try to fight this thing (sin) on your own by keeping the thing hidden, by lying to and deceiving (necessary evasive tactics) those around you whom you used to love and respect. Maybe you still do love them, but that love has become twisted. You can hope that you have the willpower to quit, but it was a lack of willpower that allowed you to get into trouble in the first place. There will be spells of remission that will only last for varying periods of time. Then back you go, repeating the failure, which will lead to increasing guilt, hardening of your heart and conscience, and more denial. This will bring not deliverance, but rather continued cycles of failure to overcome.

Third, you could choose to give up and give in. This is where you make the conscious decision to just simply embrace your sin and "go for it!" This will result in continuing hardening of your heart and conscience to the point of not caring what anyone thinks or what the consequences of this course may be. It is the ultimate selfish act of taking and keeping for yourself that which never belonged to you. You will have chosen to hold on to your sin because that is what you wanted—to give up resisting or even trying to fight back. This will lead either to hopeless despair or a callous indifference. Either way, you will be failing to overcome and win the battle. You lose even if you choose the course of "If you can't beat 'em, join 'em."

(Note: these first three choices probably will eventually result in the involuntary exposure of your behavior and character, and then you must choose between your sin and repentance. Incidentally, that is what happened to me. For more on this, see the next chapter.)

There is a fourth alternative. You can voluntarily choose to uncover yourself and your sin by confessing to someone else what you have done or been. It must be someone you trust for confidentiality reasons, but also someone who will hold you accountable. Yes, this is the most difficult choice and the hardest to perform, as it carries with it all kinds of humiliation, pain, and suffering like you have never imagined. You will make yourself vulnerable to scorn, shame, criticism, judgment, inspection, interrogation, rejection, etc. And if you are affiliated with a church body, it will probably also bring discipline and censorship, including possible excommunication. Having said all of these horrible things, this is the only honorable choice, and the only choice with any potential for overcoming your vice and restoring your wrecked life. It will involve confession, repentance, accountability, and lots of hard work to regain one of the hardest things there is to restore—trust that has been broken. It will also take a tremendous amount of time and energy to become healed and restored. But more on that later.

This confession can only happen as you become convicted before God and perhaps other humans that you are in the wrong. Conviction means agreeing with God against your sin and realizing the great offence that you have engaged in by disobeying God. It is exemplified in King David in Psalm 51:3–4: "against you, you only, have I sinned and done what is evil in your sight." The publican in Luke 18:13 said, "God, have mercy on me, a sinner!" And Job said in Job 40:4–5, "I am unworthy – how can I reply to you? I put my hand over my mouth. I spoke once, but I have no answer - twice, but I will say no more." In Job 42:2–6, Job also says, "I know that you can do all things; no plan of yours can be thwarted. You asked, 'Who is this that obscures my counsel without knowledge?' Surely I spoke of things I did not understand, things too wonderful for me to know. You said, 'Listen now, and I will speak: I will question you, and you shall answer me.' My ears have heard of you but now my eyes have seen you. Therefore I despise myself, and repent in dust and ashes!" Now that is real conviction!

Conviction and confession go hand in hand. They are the opposite of denial and hiding. Employing conviction and confession means stepping from behind the facade that your lies and necessary evasive tactics have erected. It means facing the facts and stating plainly, "Thus and thus have I done!" It means taking full responsibility for your misbehavior. In my case, I had a partner in crime. True confession required that I not even remotely try to blame her or my past (or even present) circumstances, but to accept full blame for what I had done. Any blame of any kind will diminish your taking full responsibility for your failure.

Chapter 7

Involuntary Exposure

THE PRODIGAL SON, AFTER HE had come to the end of himself in Luke 15:17, said in Luke 15:21, "Father, I have sinned against heaven, and against you. I am no longer worthy to be called your son." This kind of conviction will lead to voluntary exposure and confession.

There is also the possibility and probability that exposure will happen in an involuntary manner. It did with me, because I had not yet come to the end of myself. I had not yet given up my rights to do as I pleased, to satisfy my lustful desires. I was coasting along, wallowing in guilt, shame, depression, and deteriorating health, all the while begging God to help me (how ironic) to change my circumstances so that all this would resolve without exposure. I was unwilling to make the choice to confess and expose my sin.

Then, on June 28, 2004, it suddenly happened; I and all my dirty laundry hit the glare of broad daylight. I was exposed! It was my own personal D-day. Talk about rocking my world. I thought

I had so carefully hidden and protected it from scrutiny. Let it suffice to say that I was forced to admit the truth to my wife, who was still trusting, though it was something that she had been suspecting for quite a while.

What a shock it was to go from thinking all was covered and safe to realizing that I had to tell all. I had been caught! One might think that the truth being exposed would bring relief, and in the long run it definitely does, but at this point of involuntary exposure, there is no relief in sight. I felt as if I were a bank robber thinking he had pulled off the greatest heist, only to walk out the front door of the bank to find himself surrounded by a SWAT team in broad daylight with his hands full of stolen money. "Relief" is not the word I would use, because the truth only exposed that I was shamefully guilty of not only the sin of adultery but also lying to everyone I knew and loved. The pain and shame were overwhelming.

The worst of it was that I was not convicted to the point of turning from or giving up my sin. Although I had to admit what I had been doing, I was still embracing all of those excuses that we discussed earlier, and using painkillers (for my migraine headaches) to salve my conscience to the point of addiction to them—this in addition to my addiction to the sin of adultery. All of a sudden I was faced with the situation of being forced to make a choice between God and my sin; between my wife and my family—both immediate and extended—and my continued participation in an adulterous relationship. For many years I had enjoyed the pleasure of sin, and I was not ready to just walk away from it.

During the days leading up to my exposure, I had a premonition that something was coming, which prompted me to heighten my necessary evasive tactics, both to distract others and to attempt to escape the trap in which I found myself. The dread and threat of exposure compelled me to make a fool of myself. Truly the book of Proverbs is full of truth and wisdom. Following are some verses from that book that I should have heeded:

> He who trusts in himself is a fool. (Proverbs 28:26)

> He who conceals his sin does not prosper. (Proverbs 28:13)

> A man's own folly ruins his life. (Proverbs 19:3)

> Pride goes before destruction, a haughty spirit before a fall. (Proverbs 16:18)

> A man who commits adultery lacks judgment; whoever does so destroys himself. (Proverbs 6:32)

> Above all else, guard your heart, for it is the wellspring of life. (Proverbs 4:23)

How different things would have been if I had paid respect to and obeyed these verses, as well as chapters 5–7, which directly address the folly of adultery.

Chapter 8

Crushing/Brokenness

ONCE I WAS EXPOSED, I was immediately faced with a choice. This time it was not a choice as to whether or not to engage in evil, but rather whether or not to disengage from evil or continue to embrace it. On the surface that decision seems like a simple and straightforward choice to make. But nothing could be further from the truth, especially because I had been involved for so many years. The hooks were set pretty deeply. All of my excuses and lies that I had embraced came flooding in like a tidal wave. The walls that I had erected between my life of sin and my other life were not only very high but also very thick.

Prior to being exposed, I had rationalized everything, hardening my conscience to avoid looking at the facts of what really was at stake. It took a while for the costs that were mentioned earlier to dawn on me. Initially all that I could think of was what I would lose if I were to turn away from my failure. I was deeply enslaved and did not want to relinquish the pleasure that I *thought* my moral failure provided to me.

It took about eight days of agonizing pain and suffering—both actual physical pain and emotional pain that was indescribable— as I struggled as to whether I was going to leave my sin or embrace it. I knew it would mean giving up everything else that was important to me if I were to embrace it. It was an extremely exhausting struggle. I felt as though I was on a ledge in a deep canyon with no way out except up through a rocky chasm that was nearly vertical. I could do it God's way, which was scary and obviously difficult. The other alternative was to leap out and down into the pit of moral failure, not knowing what kind of landing was at the bottom of that canyon. There were times when it seemed as though the excuses and the foolish wrongful thinking were going to win out. Sometimes all I could do was curl up into the fetal position and plead with God to do with me what was needed. Nights were awful, as sleep eluded me most of the time. I did not know whether it would be better for God to take my life, or if he could even possibly change me. What he was doing, I later realized, was crushing me and breaking my will, which was bent on pleasing myself.

Crushing and being broken is a process by which God applies pressure by his Spirit through the Word (the Bible), through his servants, and through physical and emotional pain to bring people to the "end of themselves"—that is, to the relinquishing of their rights to self-indulgence. It is the breaking or crushing of me and my will that brought me to the point of agreeing with God about my sin and taking the side of God with regard to my moral failure. How long this process takes, God only knows. It is dependent upon one's own stubbornness, the arrogance of one's sinful flesh, and the depth and longevity of one's sinful actions.

Strangely enough, this also comes down to a choice—the choice of whether or not to willfully be broken. As painful, repulsive, and wretched the process of being broken is, I somehow knew that it was both pivotal and indispensable to the process of restoration and healing. As I allowed him to do what was needed to crush me, I eventually began begging God to crush me until all that needed to be broken was indeed crushed. I did not want to pass this way again! Obviously, this process is neither easy nor accomplished quickly. As I said, the beginning of the first phase of being broken took about eight days of misery. I say this was the first phase because it is a process that I expect and hope will continue the rest of my life. In spite of the intensity of discomfort during this process, there is a wonderful freedom in being broken and yielding my will to God's.

Essentially, three factors were instrumental in bringing me to the place of turning around, or repenting. One was faithful friends, men who cared, that came from time to time and sat with me, encouraged me, and scolded me for my wrong thinking.

Another huge factor was that my dear wife, whom I had virtually killed with my sin, rather than throwing me out, allowed me to stay in the house. Certainly I was banished from the bedroom. I spent most of my time in the basement, alone. But on the occasions when we were together upstairs, it gave me the opportunity to witness, firsthand, her pain. Witnessing that pain that I had caused was one of the factors that helped to bring me to the end of myself. I vividly remember her running to her bedroom crying hysterically and closing the door because I had tried to touch her. That is how repulsive I had become to her. I forced myself to sit in the hallway outside that door and listen to her pain that I was completely powerless to alleviate. Without her knowing it, God was using her to bring into focus the damage that I had caused by my selfish moral collapse.

My kids wrote me off, and well they might have. I certainly could not blame them. My son moved out of the house, letting me know that he had no use for me. I tell you these things not in hopes that you will feel sorry for me, but that it may help you realize the tremendous pain involved with disobedience to God's will and the effects that it has on those you love.

I remember feeling so low, so worthless, and so empty on the seventh day that I could not even feel sure that there was a God, much less one who cared about me. I expressed this empty feeling to my wife, and to my surprise, the one person I had hurt the most got up and came over and sat down on the floor next to me. She then put her arms around the man she had every right to be disgusted to touch, and just held me. At that moment she was, to me, God with skin on! I was overwhelmed, and some measure of hope was revived within me.

On the eighth day, July 6, 2004, I began reading Proverbs chapter 6. I had been reading the Bible in hope that the Scriptures by themselves would deliver me. Reading and knowing the Scriptures is not enough to save us or deliver us from anything. Unless we allow them to directly apply to our lives and behavior, and allow them to have authority over us, they will not change us. Only a right relationship with God based on *redemption* and *grace* through *faith* will provide any power to overcome the power of sin. Redemption is God paying the price for our sins and sinfulness through the death of his Son, Jesus Christ, in our place, in order to make us acceptable to him. Grace is God giving us this without our deserving it. Faith is accepting and believing that God's redemption and grace belong to us. A right relationship with God is not about being perfect, but about accepting God's gift of forgiveness.

Proverbs 5–7 discusses the sin of adultery in detail. As I read the sixth chapter, it finally dawned on me that this was a description of exactly what God thought about what I had been doing. Duh! How stubborn my heart had been. Then I read and reread chapters 5–7. Finally I came to the conclusion that I could not, and did not, want to try to face God and continue to embrace my sin. God had convicted my heart by way of faithful friends, the observance of the pain I had caused, and by the authority of the Holy Scriptures.

I at last submitted and decided to take God's side against my sin, my moral failure. As soon as I came to the choice of deciding against my adulterous relationship and seeking to follow God's will, a relief that is not possible to describe flooded my soul. I remember telling my wife that I was done with my affair and had chosen to stay with her alone, if she would have me. I did not know what she would do with that, but I remember being so happy that I was willing to do whatever it took, for as long as it took, to overcome the moral failure that had enslaved me and to rebuild the trust I had destroyed.

Later that day my good friend Mark, who had offered to walk through the mud with me, came by to check on me. The experience that I had during his visit is quite remarkable. He only had a short time, and I told him that I had chosen to agree with God against my sin. He said, "I want to pray with you, but before I do, I want to hear what God has to say to you." We both bowed our heads and sat quietly for a few minutes, a caring brother and a repentant prodigal. Mark then prayed, after which I asked him if he had heard anything from God. He said no. I told him that I had heard a voice speak very distinctly to me—a ragamuffin of the first degree. That voice said to me, "Take my hand, my child."

How huge was that? I had never heard voices before, and I have not heard any since, but this was real! Not only did God assure me that, yes, I was still his child, which I had begun to seriously doubt, but also that he would take my hand and walk up that steep, rocky canyon that lay ahead of me! Today it still sends chills up my back to think about that voice, but he has kept his word more than I could have even imagined! In Hebrews 13:5,

God says, "I will never leave you, nor forsake you." Just as in Luke 15, where the father ran to meet the Prodigal Son after he had come to the end of himself and was returning home, so he will run to meet you when you repent from your moral failure, and he will restore your soul if you are willing to submit yourself to him and be crushed and broken. "The sacrifices of God are a broken spirit; a broken and contrite heart, O God, you will not despise" (Psalm 51:17).

Chapter 9

The Road Back

I KNOW THAT YOU ARE hoping for me to give you a magic bullet that will bring everything back to "normal," whatever normal is. Sorry, but it will be neither easy nor quick. Rebuilding broken trust and changing the habits of lying and deceit take a lot of time and hard work. Remember the steep, rocky canyon that stood in front of me? See if you can envision how scary that chasm is. Some of the rocks might be loose, or I might slip and fall or just plain fail for a multitude of reasons. Most of all, it would take long, hard, strenuous work to get to the top, and I couldn't even see the top! So there were many times when I had to recall those words: "Take my hand, my child." This is similar to the need of the disciples in the boat in the storm on the Sea of Galilee who remembered the Master's words, "Let us go over to the other side." They did not need to be afraid of the storm, since Jesus Christ had stated that their destination was already settled before they embarked. Not only is there a need to rebuild others' trust in you, but you will also need to learn again to trust in God for his love and power, which are "able to do immeasurably more than we ask or imagine, according to his power that is at work within us" (Ephesians 3:20).

Remember the illustration of Achan in chapter 1, "The Anatomy of Moral Failure"? That process must be reversed by first exposing what was hidden and then restoring that which we have taken, realigning our desires. Finally, we must stop looking at or thinking about the things that led us into moral failure. Many of the rocks that I had to climb over were related to that breaking and crushing and honest exposure to which I have already referred. Some were very rough, some slippery, and others were dirty and messy. But they were in the way, and there was no way around. Another way to look at it is to realize that you have to deal with the truth and open every door to all the dirty rooms of your heart and clean out the trash that is there. If you are unwilling to open all the doors or are looking for a shortcut up the rocky canyon, then you will leave seeds of moral failure behind that will eventually bear more bad fruit! To overcome requires a thorough, ruthless exposure of all the wrong motives and desires of the heart and owning responsibility for one's failure without any excuses. Openness and honesty must become the watch words for successfully overcoming your moral failure and, ultimately, your restoration.

A pebble dropped into a pool of water creates ripples of greatest magnitude at the point of entry. Therefore, moral failure has the greatest effect on those closest to the person who failed. The closer they are, the greater the impact upon them. Conversely, the farther away they are, the less the impact. Consequently it should be obvious that there were increasing degrees of focus on those most closely impacted by my failure. I had to work hardest on myself, then my wife, then my children, my immediate family, my closest friends, my extended family, and my church body. It is not that you start and finish with one and then move on to the next, but it becomes a process whereby you may be dealing with several of these at one time. It is just that the focus of effort should be on those closest to the center of your influence. Know this right now: it will take hard work, and if you are willing to do whatever it takes, and endure whatever it takes, you will be successful. If, however, you are only willing to go halfway, then you won't even make it halfway!

There are two critical aspects of recovery that require definition. Conviction is the realization that my bad behavior is just that— categorically *bad*! It means agreeing with God that my behavior is something that he rejects and that I should reject too. It is not enough to just be convicted, as people can be convicted but not reject their behavior, even though they recognize the wrongness of their sin. Repentance, on the other hand, means not only being convicted and agreeing with God but also rejecting my bad behavior and choosing to do a 180-degree turnaround in order to head in the opposite direction.

There are signs or evidence of real repentance. It is probable that these characteristics may take time to be cultivated and to mature. First there should be a lack of defensiveness. Stop blaming others or any other things, such as circumstances. I had to take full responsibility for the bad choices I had made and for the person I had become. This point is critical, because if I had harbored any blame or resentment toward anyone for my bad choices, I would never have really become free. Remember, you must be willing to do whatever it takes—to open up any can of worms or open the doors to any dirty rooms there are in your life—if you really want progress. This is why the crushing and breaking are so vital to becoming free. Not until my will was broken and I was willing to do whatever it took to expose and uncover anything was I able to begin the long trek up that steep and rocky canyon to recovery and overcoming the wrong behavior in my life.

Scripture is full of examples. King David said, "I have sinned and done evil in thy sight" (Psalm 51:4). Achan said, "Thus and thus have I done ..." (Joshua 7:9–12). Jonah said, "I know that it is my fault" (Jonah 1:12). Job said, "I am unworthy – how can I reply to you? I put my hand over my mouth. I spoke once, but I have no answer – twice, but I will say no more ... Therefore, I despise myself and repent in dust and ashes" (Job 40:4–5; 42:5–6). Job was someone whom God called "a blameless and upright man, who fears God and shuns evil" (Job 1:8).

Peter, after denying his Lord and Master and receiving a look from Jesus, "went outside and wept bitterly" (Luke 22:62).

The Prodigal Son, "when he came to his senses [The KJV renders this as "when he came to the end of himself"], he said, 'I will set out and go back to my father (180-degree turnaround—repentance] and say to him: Father, I have sinned against heaven and against you. I am no longer worthy to be called your son' … so he got up and went to his father" (Luke 15:17–20). There is so much here in this story! He is crushed and broken, coming to the end of himself. There is confession and repentance, all accompanied by action on his part without him blaming anyone but himself. So now you know where I got the expression "come to the end of yourself."

I was encouraged to climb that steep and rocky canyon because of those reassuring words: "Take my hand my child!" But there were also written words from the Holy Scriptures that lighted and pointed the way. The first are in Jeremiah 18:3–4: "So I went down to the potter's house, and I saw him working at the wheel. But the pot he was shaping from the clay was marred in his hands; so the potter formed it into another pot, shaping it as seemed best to him." First, where was the pot when it was marred? It was in the potter's hands. It never left his hands and was never out of his control. Next the lump of clay had to be crushed and completely reformed into a new lump so that the potter could make it into another pot as it seemed best to the potter, not the pot. It was such a relief for me when I realized that I was in his hands—even during my crash on the rocks, my marring—and that he was going to use this process to bring about a new pot that suited him better than before. Boasting only

49

in the grace of God, I know that he has made me much more useful to him and his purposes now than I ever could have been had I not been crushed and made new.

In the gospel of John, chapter 8, a woman was caught in the act of adultery. She was brought before Jesus to be judged by him. Rather than judge her, he convicted her accusers, who had to depart with their guilty consciences, leaving her in the presence of Jesus. "Jesus straightened up and asked her, 'Woman, where are they? Has no one condemned you?' 'No one, sir,' she said. 'Then neither do I condemn you,' Jesus declared, 'Go now and leave your life of sin'" (John 8:10–11). First there is forgiveness, and then he instructs her to repent (leave her life of sin). Which brings me back to the idea that we can change, we can repent, we can overcome! Some will ask, "Can we really change?" Well, Jesus would never have asked her or you or me to do the impossible!

In Psalm 51:17, after King David confesses and repents, he says; "The sacrifices of God are a broken spirit; a broken and contrite heart, O God, you will not despise." Please read this whole Psalm, as it is the right response of a man who has committed adultery and is in the process of overcoming his moral failure. There is much to be learned in these words of a truly convicted and repentant man.

I say all of this to show that even though we mess up, God is willing to forgive us where there is genuine conviction, brokenness, confession, and repentance. All of this is foundational to overcoming sin and being restored to a useful life and the enjoyment of freedom. It should be understood that while some moral failure will leave permanent scars, there is still the real possibility for life to be better than it was before, if we are only willing to do the hard work of climbing that steep and rocky canyon, trusting in the One for whom nothing is impossible.

Chapter 10

Uncovering—Exposure

U SING THE ANATOMY OF MORAL failure—looking, coveting, taking, and hiding—I want to show the way up that steep, rocky canyon by reversing that process. That means hiding will need to be addressed first. The opposite of hiding is obviously exposure or uncovering. In this context, this refers to the exposure and confession of our sin to those whom we have offended. This begins with (and probably has already begun to happen if there has been genuine conviction and repentance) the process of stopping the lying to yourself. Granted, this is a process that takes time, consistency, and persistence. You must make a complete inventory of your failings to yourself.

Yes, this is painful and requires a huge amount of personal integrity, which is something that those of us who have committed moral failure have in very short supply. After all, a lack of integrity is an integral component of moral failure. This is where you may require deep, often painful, introspection as well as outside help, such as that from a friend or counselor, to help you dig out the ugly truth about yourself. I found help from all of those but also from the Scripture found in James 1:5–8: "If any of you lacks wisdom, he should ask God, who gives generously to all without finding fault, and it will be given unto him. But when he asks, he must believe and not doubt, because he who doubts is like a wave of the sea, blown and tossed by the wind. That man should not think he will receive anything from the Lord; he is a double-minded man, unstable in all he does."

This passage has been a huge help to me, but it may require some explanation. When those of us who lack wisdom come to God in faith, believing that he exists and is willing to reward us for seeking him, he will give us the wisdom that we need generously. We must come with the attitude of being willing to do whatever it is God shows us to do. However, if we come to him with our own agenda and have already decided what we want, that means we are doubting God's motive; this unbelief will result in no help from God. Don't make the mistake of thinking that God is dumb or wrong. He never is dumb or wrong, and he also is aware of all that is in your heart, as well as all that you are and have done. You cannot fool him.

This brings me to an illustration. Suppose an exterminator is called in to eliminate some pest from your home. He is going to want access to every room, drawer, and cubby hole. Any place that has been accessible to those pests must be opened. No room can be left closed; all must be exposed to the light of God's searchlight and to the appraisal of those whom you invite to help.

Remember the ripple effect of the pebble in the pool of water? After you have become honest with yourself, then the scope of uncovering must widen. Perhaps it is obvious, but your spouse is next, if you have one, and then children, parents, and any other immediate family. As time goes on, the circle of influence may be widened to include others. But be cautious regarding being overzealous about confession, as it may lead to unnecessary pain and innuendo that could otherwise be avoided.

This is not an "I messed up and it will never happen again" confession. Rather, it means naming specifically what you have done, or failed to do—a renouncement of that bad behavior. Make no misleading statements as to the severity of your failure. By all means, you must take complete ownership of that failure; that is, do not blame anyone or anything else in any way, shape, or form. This is your problem, and you must accept full responsibility. Not every sordid detail must be discussed, but no one should be misled by minimizing what you have done. Remember, recovery is about the truth, not more lies or misleading statements. While details are not important, an honest description of the nature and duration of the offence is! It is the confession of all that has been wrongly embraced, of all that has been yielded to, and of all that has had dominion or control over you. Proverbs 28:13 says, "He who conceals his sins does not prosper, but whoever confesses and renounces them finds mercy."

This first step is very difficult because it will probably come as a shock to many, and you have no way of knowing how people will respond to finding out that you have not been what they thought you were, much less how despicable you have become. On the other hand, it may surprise you how gracious some people will be because they know that they have the same potential for wrongdoing as you have. These are the real people and the ones whom you should cultivate as friends.

Beware of and discount the opinion of any who feel that they could never fall to the depths of your sin. They are lying to themselves, just as the religious leaders of Jesus' day did. See Luke 10, which is the parable of the good samaritan. In that parable, the priest and the Levite pass by on the other side of the road from the needy man. In John 8, those religious leaders brought to Jesus a woman whom they had caught in the act of adultery, wanting him to condemn her. Instead, he convicted them. He used the strongest words of condemnation for those who thought they were righteous but were hypocrites.

I vividly remember telling two friends that were working at my place what I had done. They both came and put their arms around me, saying, "You are no worse than us, as we could have easily done the same thing!" Not everyone will respond similarly, but a huge number of them did in my case. It is true that there were those who reacted in disgust, which was justified and was what I expected and deserved. After all, I was disgusted with myself. Many of those who did react negatively eventually became more cordial as I continued to do whatever it took. Some of them have even become good friends again—in some cases better friends than before. Realize that what you have done has broken the trust that these people have placed in you; uncovering your sin will reveal that to them. In many cases it will hurt them deeply, and you must give them space to vent their hurt, frustration, and anger. The way they react is their business. It is your responsibility to be open, honest, and understanding, and to be willing to do whatever it takes to regain that trust, however long it may take. You broke that trust; they did not.

As I said before, do not make the promise that this will never happen again. You do not know that, and in order to be truthful you must not engage in statements that might not be true. Most people who have failed have, at one time or another, experienced some degree of relapse. There will be more on relapses later.

This openness and honesty have to become a change in your lifestyle, as it has become ingrained in your being to lie and to hide. It will become necessary to catch yourself immediately in the smallest distortion of the truth and correct it. You will also become aware that it is very freeing not to have to employ those necessary evasive tactics that you have become so adept at. Then you will become startled to find the liberty that the truth brings with it. See John 8:32, 36.

Even your relationships with others will become less strained as you continue to be truthful. The funny thing is that if people learn that they can trust someone who has dreadfully broken their trust, they will experience marked improvement in that relationship. But it requires dogged persistence, as some take much longer than others to be convinced. The good news is that you will find some who will see and acknowledge the change from deceit to honesty and will embrace you wholeheartedly. This encouragement should be taken seriously, valued, and treasured. This is exactly where we want to go, and the end result will be worth every moment and ounce of effort spent. Yes, it is hard work, but isn't everything that is worthwhile worth working hard for?

Chapter 11

Damage Repair

WHEN WE STEAL SOMETHING FROM someone and want to make it right, that thing that we stole needs to be returned, if possible. Taking what does not belong to us is not always confined to the theft of objects. One can steal time, steal affection, take inappropriate liberties, trash someone else's life or reputation, cheat at something, cheat on someone, or grasp and embrace something to which one is not entitled. Whenever we choose to take or embrace that which we should not, we are embarking upon a course of moral failure, which will eventually lead to us being enslaved by that failure. When this is the case, we are choosing wrongly.

In many ways, irreversible damage can be brought about by moral failure. A child can be created or lost, money can be lost, reputations can be damaged, and personal relationships can be destroyed, including marriages and families. The list goes on and on. Alcoholism and other addictions, such as addictions to drugs, food, gambling, and computer games and other high-tech stuff can cause permanent damage. Anything that takes away from someone else's time or substance is theft.

The first thing we must do is let go of whatever it is that we have wrongly taken. If possible, we must restore or repay the debt. Materially we may not be able to return that which we have taken. What is gone is gone. But that does not mean that we can do nothing to reverse the taking process. If it can't be returned, or if payment can't be made to replace that which was taken, then we must be prepared to make investments or deposits toward those whom we have damaged or hurt. Dr. Willard Harley Jr., a noted psychologist and author, has used the example of a "Love Bank" to illustrate this notion. Dr. Harley says, "You and I have within us a Love Bank, and each person we know has an account in it. The Love Bank helps us keep track of the way people treat us. When people do things that make us feel good, 'love units' are deposited, and when they do things that make us feel bad, love units are withdrawn" (From *Surviving An Affair*, pg. 34). (Read any of his books [e.g., *His Needs Her Needs*]; they are great. Dr. Harley has a unique program of marriage building. See marriagebuilders. com.) If I have fallen into moral failure, I will seriously begin to deplete the balance in the love bank of any of those with whom I have a relationship. When I become exposed, my respective love banks are badly in the red, as I have just made massive withdrawals from the love banks of everyone I know.

So what is to be done? Confession and exposure have occurred, so now begins the really hard and tedious work. The steep, rocky canyon appears almost vertical when I contemplate the massive debt I owe. How do I restore the balance to those love banks that I have depleted? Sincere confession and apology are obvious ways to do so, and they require humility and willingness to accept full personal responsibility. That leaves no room for blame or excuses. Openness and honesty are necessary, but not excessive details.

Remember that repentance is a 180-degree turn. There is no way that a promise to be different is going to hold any water with others, because everything that you said in the past regarding the failure that you have embraced has been a lie. It is only by being different that anyone will believe in you again. Only time and continued persistence in letting go, taking the humble path, and exhibiting a willingness to do whatever it takes will make significant deposits in those love banks. Demonstrating that you have taken definite steps to distance yourself from whatever it is that has captured or enslaved your affections and desires, as well as making a demonstrable effort to avoid any further temptations, are the only ways of evidencing real change to others. Remember that blame or excuses do not create deposits; they simply make further withdrawals from those accounts.

When you openly and honestly confess and apologize, taking full responsibility without blaming anyone or anything (such as past circumstances), the response of compassion that many will exhibit toward you may surprise you. There will be those self-righteous souls who will not be placated by anything you do. Let them go. Doggedly pursue a pathway of demonstrating that not only are you done with your failure but also that you are reconstructing your life to avoid further wrong choices. Realize that it may take months or even years to restore the balance in those love banks, and some even may never allow you to make deposits. The change in your life and attitude, however, will soften even some of the hardest of hearts. Many will see the change and get on board with forgiving you.

Restitution is difficult because, in so many cases, that which has been taken is intangible. That is why it requires a quiet, humble owning of your failure, the assumption of full responsibility, and a sincere apology accompanied by a consistent demonstration of a change in your behavior. Some of the Scriptures that have been a help to me are Proverbs 15:1, 28 (the whole chapter, but especially verse 13), and Psalm 51 (the whole psalm, but especially verse 17).

Chapter 12

Coveting—Realignment of Desires

THESE ARE ALL VERSES THAT address desires and God's perspective on them:

- Ephesians 2:3
- 1 Corinthians 14:1
- Galatians 4:9
- James 4:2–10
- 1 Peter 2:2

As we continue on our journey to reverse moral failure, we come to the subject of coveting, or desiring. It is interesting that Colossians 3:5 says, "Put to death, therefore, whatever belongs to your earthly nature: sexual immorality, impurity, lust, evil desires and greed [covetousness] which is idolatry." Another definition of covetousness is "unrestrained or unbridled desire." First Corinthians 12:31 instructs us to eagerly desire (covet earnestly) the best gifts (love). Love is the opposite of selfishness, the basic ingredient to moral failure. In order to fall into moral failure of any kind, we must allow our natural desires to operate without hindrance. In some cases it is not only natural desires but also unnatural evil desires that are innate within each of us. In order to reverse the process of moral failure, we must realign our desires with those desires that are consistent with making right choices. As a Christian, I had to bring my behavioral choices into line with God's opinion, as found in his Word.

We must realize that we are naturally endowed with evil and fleshly desires. Ephesians 2:1–3 says, "As for you, you were dead in your transgressions and sins, in which you used to live when you followed the ways of this world and of the ruler of the kingdom of the air, the spirit who is now at work in those who are disobedient. All of us also lived among them at one time, gratifying the cravings of our sinful nature and following its desires and thoughts." We need to kill the desires inside of us that are causing our selfish behavior that is hurting those around us. That is, we must treat those desires as dead and having no power any longer. It is helpful if we can realize what desires we have turned loose in our lives so that we know what to address. This takes brutal honesty with ourselves (we must stop lying to ourselves) and self-discipline to put these desires under restraint and say no to them, rather than to allow them to take control of our behavior and dictate that we act immorally.

We can't just say no to what is morally wrong; we must at the same time learn to say yes to what is morally right. If we just close out some immoral aspect of our lives without replacing it with what is appropriate, we will replace it with more and worse evil. This principle is illustrated in Luke 11:24–26: "When an evil spirit comes out of a man, it goes through arid places seeking rest and does not find it … 'I will return to the house I left.' When it arrives, it finds the house swept clean and put in order. Then it goes and takes seven other spirits more wicked than itself, and they go in and live there. And the final condition of that man is worse than the first." In Colossians 3:5–14 we are told to get rid of the evil in our lives and to clothe ourselves with that which is right. Psalm 119:37 and Proverbs 4:15 both express the need of turning away from evil toward good. If we can learn to say no to evil and yes to that which is good, then we will really be on the way to reversing the process of moral failure.

Chapter 13

Looking in the Right Direction

THE FIRST ACTION THAT LED us down the wrong road to moral failure was entertaining a look. Envisioning evil is the first step to embracing evil. If I don't see it, or if I inadvertently do see it but do not engage in contemplation of the evil, then I will not take the next step to coveting or desiring that evil. This, again, requires self-discipline. It either protects me from exposure to temptation, or if temptation arises beyond my control, it allows me to distance myself from it as much as possible. Joseph was confronted with temptation in the form of Potiphar's wife in Genesis 39:7–12. He ran away and put distance between himself and temptation. Yes, you may say that it cost him a prison sentence, but God was in control and eventually used his prison circumstance to deliver not only him but also the nation of Egypt and, ultimately, Potiphar's whole family from starvation. In Proverbs 4:23–27, there is some sage advice: "Above all else, guard your heart, for it is the wellspring of life … Let your eyes look straight ahead, fix your gaze directly before you. Make level paths for your feet and take only ways that are firm. Do not swerve to the right or the left; keep your foot from evil." Looking at what is appropriate helps us avoid looking at what is not.

In particular, it is imperative that we distance ourselves from the opportunity that might afford us a look at that which could wrongly attract our affections and desires. This is not a once-and-done experience, but a daily and momentary diligence to separate ourselves from contemplating anything that would lead us astray. In this day and age it is becoming more difficult, due to modern media and technology, to avoid seeing things that may defile or tempt us. Just remember, our lives are the results of the choices we make.

Chapter 14

Get Help and Drop the Excuses

S O FAR WE HAVE DISCUSSED what you personally can and should do. Perhaps you think that you can do this. Or worse yet, perhaps you think you can apply these principles by yourself and no one will be the wiser. No, no, no! This is a shortcut that avoids exposure and will result in disaster. It is such a temptation to fix this without exposure, and frankly that is part of what took me so long to get deliverance. While there may be a very, very few individuals who can turn off making those bad choices, the whopping majority got into this mess because of some character flaw or weakness and will need help—lots of help—to recover. In the chapter on exposure I pointed out that we first of all need to get right with God, as he is the one we have most greatly offended. While that is very true, I have to say that that will not be enough. I knew that God knew all about my failure, and I confessed to him and repented many times. The problem with that is that it does not require accountability or provide for damage repair to those who have been hurt. The tendency for relapse is greatly increased if no one else besides you and God knows about your failure. This goes back to the metaphor of the exterminator having access to every room of your life that your moral failure may have infected.

Please don't use the excuse that you just can't help it and that you will always be a mess. As I stated in the introduction, that is the main reason I am writing this book. You can overcome! As I told you earlier, I was invited to a men's retreat by one of my mentors and asked to share my story. Later a man approached me, and to make a long story short, he said, "Once you have tasted it [in his case, adultery], you never lose the urge … it is always there whenever you see an attractive woman." That is a bald-faced lie. It is just a big, fat excuse to not do the hard work and face your failure, open all the doors, accept the blame and responsibility, and do whatever it takes to break the cycle. There are countless numbers of excuses for not overcoming and falling backward into the mud. You don't need me to help you find any more by listing things; that would require a whole other book. Suffice it to say that you made a bad choice and need to make the right choice to face it and do whatever it takes.

For the remainder of this book, I am going to make the assumption that you are done with excuses and blame and are taking full responsibility, having confessed and repented from your moral failure.

Chapter 15

Mentoring and Accountability

ONCE YOU HAVE DECIDED TO climb up the steep, rocky canyon to recovery and overcoming, there are two overwhelmingly important issues that really go together. They are mentoring and accountability, and you can't have one without the other. There is also one very important requirement for those involved in mentoring and accountability, and that is confidentiality.

I can't stress confidentiality enough, because if you are not sure of confidentiality, there is no way that you can be open and honest. And you must be completely open and honest with anyone that is going to be in the position of helping you. Yes, you will need help—and badly. The situation is like quicksand; the more you struggle by your own efforts, the more mired down you become. You need someone with his or her feet on firm ground, someone that you can trust implicitly to throw you a lifeline and haul you out. It still remains that you must secure the lifeline around yourself by making right choices, regardless of how difficult or costly they may be.

Speaking of mentors, I am reminded of Galatians 6:1–3: "Brothers, if someone is caught in a sin, you who are spiritual should restore him gently. But watch yourself, or you also may be tempted. Carry each other's burdens, and in this way you will fulfill the law of Christ. If anyone thinks he is something when he is nothing, he deceives himself." This passage is very instructive for those who would aspire to the honor of mentoring a fallen brother, but it is also helpful to the one who has been ensnared by a sin. Look for someone who is not above realizing his own potential to fall into a trap of his own, though it may be another sin, different from yours. I found it very difficult to trust those who found themselves without fault. At the same time, however, I found it relatively easy to trust those who were very aware of their own shortcomings. All of the brothers who were of significant help to me revealed their flaws and the temptations to which they were susceptible. That required that they be able to trust me too. How is that for grace? Some may think that they are spiritual, but they may be too proud to own their faults. In other words, they think they are something when they are nothing. Stay away from them, however well-meaning they may seem. They will not help to carry your burden, because they can't and won't understand your difficulty. Don't look for the most religious or prestigious person either, as he or she may be just like the priest and Levite, who, when they saw the man in the ditch in the parable of the good samaritan in Luke 10:25–37, walked by on the other side. You will need someone who is willing to come down into the mud with you and share your pain and suffering, to listen compassionately, and to tell you the truth gently but firmly.

When I look back at this period in my life, it is sort of a blur, and yet there are things that are still crystal clear. There was one man with whom I had had a great relationship before, and he had tried many times to get me to acknowledge what I am sure he knew was the truth. Just before my exposure, I flat out lied to him about the nature of my relationship with the other woman, in response to his direct questioning. After my exposure, he sat in my living room and told me straight-out what he thought of me and my behavior. Then he told me that he loved me and would walk through the mud with me as long as I needed him. What a friend!

As I told you in chapter 8, he stopped by on the afternoon of the eighth day of my valley of death, and I had finally come to the end of myself. I told him of my decision to agree with God's appraisal of my sinful behavior and my desire to repent and change directions. I told him I was afraid and scared about what was ahead. He was short on time but wanted to pray with me before he left. Before he prayed, he said that he wanted us to be still and hear what the Lord had to say to me. We sat quietly for a few moments, and then he prayed. I asked him if he had heard anything at all from God. He said that he had not. Now, I am about as conservative as you can imagine—well, maybe not politically, but doctrinally I am. I had to tell him that I had heard a voice during that time of quiet listening; It had said to me, "Take my hand, my child." Even now it brings tears to my eyes as I write this to you. I was overwhelmed, as I had never heard God speak before and have not heard him speak since. There I was, facing that steep, rocky canyon, feeling helpless and weak, and my greatest mentor and accountability partner who had just volunteered was the almighty God!

God continued to use my friend for many years, and we have had sweet fellowship together, though not often enough. But I can't tell you what a comfort it was for God to let me know that I was still his child in spite of the horrible dishonor that I had brought on him and my loved ones, and that he wanted me to take hold of his hand so he could help me to walk up that seemingly impassible, steep, rocky canyon to the end.

Of course I can't know what, if any, relationship you have with God, but I have found that picking up the pieces of moral failure and overcoming is much easier when God is on your side. As it was, God used several principal men in my life, as well as many others. I could not possibly name them all, so all of them will remain anonymous. I could never have overcome my failure alone. I doubt very seriously that you can either. Essentially there were three main ones that helped me. The one I mentioned in the previous paragraph was the first, but time became an issue. Another friend, from our Bible study group, asked a semiretired pastor at the church we had been attending to get involved. This pastor was well experienced in counseling and so seemed to be a good potential resource for me. We determined that we would meet weekly for eighteen months. Today, nine years later, we still meet weekly and are best friends. At this point I am sure that the relationship is no longer one-sided, but a mutually beneficial situation.

Later on I met for a couple of years with a younger pastor at the church we now attend. It was that pastor who reintroduced me to teaching the word in an adult Bible study and, eventually, doing some fill-in preaching on Sundays at other churches. God's grace exceeded whatever I might have imagined by using these men of God to refine and remold my life. They were men prepared by God to help me spiritually.

Notice I have not even mentioned the psychological counseling in which my wife and I had to participate. That is a whole other investment. But remember, you have to be willing to do whatever it takes. Ephesians 3:20–21 says, "Now unto him who is able to do immeasurably more that all we ask or imagine, according to his power that is at work in us, to him be glory in the church and in Christ Jesus throughout all generations, forever and ever! Amen." That glory in the church is God using his people to do his work. Don't tell me it is hopeless; I know better—much better! There are people God has prepared to help you before you even know they are doing so.

Chapter 16

What Does it Take?

H OW DOES IT WORK? FIRST of all, you must realize your need of help and resolve to use the help that you find with candid openness and honesty. Do I sound like a broken record? There is good reason for that. Whether they are pastors, counselors, close friends, psychologists, or even relatives, you need these people. They may come on their own volition, or you may have to seek them out. Regardless, it is your mess, and you have to clean it up. So start looking for confidential listeners and confidential truth tellers. Your church body may be well equipped to handle your problem, or poorly equipped. Don't count on that; you need individuals of great integrity, wherever you may find them. In my case the first friend I mentioned earlier, the one who prayed with me the time I heard the voice, is still a faithful friend and would not hesitate to knock the air out of me if he was suspicious of anything.

I continue to meet with my retired pastor friend. The pastor at the church we now attend felt that I had made enough progress that he finally put me back to work, teaching in the adult Bible study group. What grace! Did we see professional counselors? Yes! My wife and I traveled out of town weekly for two-hour sessions with a counselor for almost a year till we felt we had reached a limit of benefit. We went through two other professional counselors. I also had a brother-in-law who periodically called me from across the country. Really, you need to avail yourself of whatever help is at your disposal. Take all you can get and all you can afford. There will never be a better investment that you can make.

It is interesting that the one I had offended the most, my wife, Mary, was my best friend, counselor, and truth teller. She allowed me the privilege of staying in our home, which provided me with a firsthand perspective of the damage I had caused. Our youngest daughter was already married and out of the house. Our oldest daughter stayed at home for two to three weeks till she could not stand it anymore. Our youngest child was our son, who left in obvious and well-deserved disgust without even having a place to go. How necessarily humiliating! The love bank that was the most depleted belonged to my wife. I had to become completely transparent with her. I had to let her know where I was at all times. If I spoke to someone on the phone, I made an account of it. My life had to become an open book to her. I hope that this does not sound too tough for you, as it was a privilege to be given a second chance to restore a debt by making deposits in her love bank and rebuilding her trust. I was willing to do whatever it took to restore the tremendous debt that I created. My wife was in such a distracted state that I had to fix meals for her. I am not much of a cook, but then she was not all that hungry. But every little thing that I could do for her was like balm to my soul. I requested her to decide what it would take and then sought with all my heart to fulfill her requests. No more hiding, lying, or deceiving of any kind was permitted. Old habits die hard! Recognition of those habits and confession and repentance began to allow healing to begin and progress. Was it slow? Yes, very slow, but though it seemed interminable, progress was being made.

You are probably asking how long it takes. That is a question that frequented my mind. There is no answer to that question, but as you might have guessed, my answer is "As long as it takes!" Now, I am not so naive as to think that every marriage can be saved, because it takes two willing hearts. But if both parties are willing to do the hard work to evaluate themselves, with the help of others, it can be done!

Whether or not your relationships can be restored, you can overcome your moral failure. You can and you must, whether or not your loved ones come alongside you. Never let anyone tell you differently. It is important that it be understood that it is you that needs fixing, not your spouse, your dad, your mom, your boss, or any other person (though they may need help too). Otherwise, you begin blaming others and deny accepting full responsibility. If you will trust this process, you can overcome, but more often than not, those around you will step up and take responsibility too. You can only lead by example, not by giving direction, because you forfeited that right when you used bad judgment and chose wrongly. This is not to say others do not need to be fixed, but rather to say that you can only take responsibility for yourself. Others must take responsibility for themselves. If there are relational complications, outside help or therapy will probably be needed, either together, separately, or both.

Chapter 17

The Truth Will Set You Free

Accountability is a tough and sensitive issue. If you are engaging in moral failure for any length of time, you will become an expert at lying to yourself and to others, and you will become a master of deceit by using necessary evasive tactics. The longer you are involved, the more proficient you will become! Consequently, telling the truth does not come automatically, but deceit does come naturally. In fact, any time there is a potential for anything that might be accusatory, we automatically shift into a defensive mode or into an avoidance behavior. This is why it is a requirement to do whatever it takes, no matter what the personal costs, to learn to tell the truth consistently. There will be the temptation to twist or embellish the truth or to omit some detail, depending on how we want to influence the impression of our audience. As a result of this ingrained deceit, it is highly important, if you want to succeed in overcoming, that you choose to be accountable to those who are willing to ask the hard questions and not back down when you are reverting to blowing smoke at them by fudging the truth. A willingness to be open and honest is a true sign of an authentic desire to overcome and become healthy again. If there are some areas of your life that you are not willing to be open about, then I seriously doubt you are really serious about recovery and restoration. Accountability is all about the naked truth. As John 8:32 says, "The truth will set you free."

The foundation of sin is deceitfulness. We despise the Word of the Lord and lie to ourselves, which leads to embracing our sin and doing what is evil in God's eyes. Soon it will become an ongoing cycle of deceit, sin, lies, more deceit, more sin, and on and on. Ultimately, while we are lying to ourselves, embracing a sinful pathway of bondage, we are despising God himself. At the root of this deceit is pride—pride in my own judgment and my own power to control my life without any regard to God's claims upon me. As Proverbs 14:27 states, "The fear of the Lord is a fountain of life, turning a man from the snares of death."

Chapter 18

Relapses

R ELAPSES CAN AND DO HAPPEN. When that occurs, the trust level that has been rebuilt gets blown up and destroyed. Hence we find ourselves back at square one, but hopefully now you know what to do. Return to openness by honest confession. Realize that you relapsed because either the systems of recovery were not strong enough or you didn't thoroughly repent. Because of this, you need a brutally honest self-appraisal of the depth of your confession and repentance, made on your knees. You must also make sure you are done with your sin and are turning completely away. Then you must strengthen those systems of recovery. You will need to spend more time with those who are your mentors and or accountability partners. You may even need to add a partner. Find a tough one. You must be more open and more honest than ever before—more transparent. In a word, you have to be even more accountable.

Does the experience of a relapse mean you have lost the fight? The answer is a resounding no. You have lost everything if you give up the fight and give in to your cravings. A relapse demonstrates that you have found a loophole that must be closed. It means that you have lost ground that will need to be regained, but it can be regained if you are willing to do whatever it takes. It may require a reassessment of the level of openness, honesty, confession, and repentance from the beginning. A relapse is a signal of how necessary it is to be rigidly vigilant and to maintain an adequate distance from the temptation in order to prevent contact. Remember that seeing leads to contemplation and, on down the road, to coveting, taking, and hiding.

Overcoming moral failure is like building a wall. The longer you spend building it, the higher, thicker, and stronger it becomes. If there is a breach in that wall, it must be repaired as soon and as quickly as possible, because it will not function as a wall of separation for anything. Keep at it long enough and you will eventually have a fortress. But even a fortress can be climbed over, and so it remains that we must never forget what Jeremiah 17:9 says: "The heart is deceitful above all things." Nor can we forget what is said in Proverbs 28:26: "He that trusts in himself is a fool, but he who walks in wisdom is kept safe!" The fact that you were once entrapped by moral failure, or worse yet have relapsed after escaping, only proves the truth of these words. Never, ever trust yourself!

Chapter 19

Rooms with Closed Doors

I MUST SAY ONE MORE word about secret areas or rooms of our lives, to which we are unwilling to open up the doors for others. If such is the case, if there is even one room that you are not willing to open the door to in order to let someone see what is there, then you are still in bondage, and all the mentoring, accountability, therapy, or whatever will not bring recovery. There is no recovery without complete openness and honesty. There must be complete candor with those whom you have offended and with those who are trying to help you. If you are not willing to open every door, don't waste other people's time by pretending. Even worse is the excuse of not opening doors because you think you can fix it yourself so that no one will know about your dirty little secret(s). The other idea that is all wrong is the idea that if you could just get your relationship with others and especially with God right, then you would become empowered to overcome. This does not work. I tried for years. It all goes back to complete brokenness and coming to the end of yourself.

It is inevitable that, even though we are children of God, redeemed by the blood of Christ, we will struggle against sin. There are two long passages of Scripture that I will only reference here. Romans 7:7–24 and 1 John chapter 1. In that struggle against sin, we have the opportunity to judge ourselves. First Corinthians 11:31 says, "But if we judged ourselves, we would not come under judgment." The alternative is to choose not to judge ourselves, so that we can continue to embrace our wrong choices. If you refuse self-judgment, then your life will bear the miserable fruits of sin. Hebrews 12:6 states, "The Lord disciplines those he loves, and he punishes everyone he accepts as a son." There is only one path to freedom, and it is not through denial or deceit. It is through the truth and only the truth. Please don't hold back and refuse to let the light of God's Word search every room in your heart. If you do, you will remain stuck in the mire of failure!

Chapter 20

Benefits of Overcoming Moral Failure

IN CHAPTER 2 WE DISCUSSED the costs of moral failure. It is only fitting that we end this discussion with the benefits of overcoming moral failure. Essentially, the benefits of overcoming moral failure are the opposite of the effects of moral failure. The costs and effects of moral failure are monumental, so the benefits to overcoming are numerous as well.

Overcoming moral failure will result in clearer thought and the ability to come to right conclusions. You will begin to trust your own judgment, as will those around you. You may not think that is possible, but it is. You will stop being the fool that lacks judgment, because you have judged yourself and condemned the bad behavior.

It will take a while for the suffering to dissipate, but instead of making love bank withdrawals, you will be able to make deposits in the love banks of those important to you. You will suddenly realize that you yourself are not suffering as much as when you were entrapped.

You will probably be surprised by the amount of time and money that you wasted. You will experience an increase in available time and income for the benefits of others as well as yourself. Time and money that were once spent destructively now can be engaged with constructive and rejuvenating activities. The things that matter can now take priority!

What a relief it is to stop the necessary evasive tactics! No longer is there a need to lie, cover up, deceive, and evade the truth. Remember, the truth will, indeed, set you free. The freedom from the need for evasion is enormous.

When you stop lying, especially to yourself, you will automatically experience a reduction in stress and deterioration. This will result in all kinds of health benefits in body, soul, mind, and spirit. If you have engaged in any substance abuse, this improvement of health and well-being will be profound.

The sense of guilt, shame, and failure will be diminished, especially as you realize what the redemption that God provides through his Son, Jesus Christ, has accomplished. It can really set you at liberty in the righteousness of God in Christ Jesus. "But now a righteousness from God, apart from law, has been made known, to which the Law and the Prophets testify. This righteousness from God comes through faith in Jesus Christ to all who believe. There is no difference, for all have sinned and fall short of the glory of God, and are justified freely by his grace through the redemption that came by Christ Jesus" (Romans 3:21–24).

There will be a sense of triumph as you trust in God and obey him. The realization of victory may take a while in coming, but as you immerse yourself in the grace of God, it will indeed lead to complete restoration and freedom.

Emotional and spiritual health will be restored as you fill yourself with the truth and walk in it. You will begin to see clearly what is right and wrong and begin to make choices that coincide with the will of God. This, in turn, will help to restore the dignity and self-esteem that you lost when you did those things you were ashamed of and felt so guilty about.

Overcoming moral failure brings with it empowerment. "I can do everything through him who gives me strength" (Philippians 4:13). This means that when other temptations cross your path, and they will, you hold a confidence in God that this, too, can be conquered.

Now instead of being entrapped and enslaved by the thing that you know is wrong, you have the freedom to choose what is right and to be the person God intended you to be. "It is for freedom that Christ has set us free. Stand firm, then, and do not let yourselves be burdened again by a yoke of slavery" (Galatians 5:1).

Where there was collateral damage, now there can be collateral blessing. Instead of hurting and causing pain to those close to you, you can invest in promoting their happiness.

Those relationships that you destroyed can now begin to be restored and rebuilt. True, this takes time—lots of time—and lots of hard work, but you must be willing to do whatever it takes. There is no limit to the efforts that true repentance will stimulate.

As you begin to rebuild and restore these broken relationships to make deposits in bankrupt love banks, you will slowly experience an increase in trust and respect. Who can place a value on trust, love, and respect? It will not come automatically just because someone says, "I forgive you." It must be earned, and it takes time to prove the reality of that repentance.

Above all else, overcoming moral failure will make it possible to be in a right relationship with the God, whom you have put at a distance.

> If we claim to have fellowship with him [God] yet walk in the darkness, we lie and do not live by the truth. But if we walk in the light, as he is in the light, we have fellowship with one another, and the blood of Jesus, his son, purifies us from all sin. If we claim to be without sin, we deceive ourselves and the truth is not in us. If we confess our sins, he is faithful and just and will forgive us our sins and purify us from all unrighteousness. If we claim we have not sinned, we make him out to be a liar and his word has no place in our lives. (1 John 1:6–10)

Being in a right relationship with God will make it possible, and is requisite, to be in a right relationship with those around you. Moral failure brings in separation, but overcoming will bridge the gap and bring you back into the enjoyment of life and liberty. Don't you want to love and be in the enjoyment of the love of both God and those close to you? The God that created you did so in order that you might have fellowship with him. He also said it was not good that man should be alone, and he encourages us to "consider how we may spur one another on toward love and good deeds" (Hebrews 10:24). All of this can only happen when you come to the end of pleasing yourself and turn to God for his help and redemption. Like the Prodigal Son when he came to the end of himself, the Father will run to meet you and throw a party: "For this son of mine was dead, and is alive again; he was lost and is found, so they began to celebrate" (Luke 15:24).

The bottom line is that you can—with the help of God, his Holy Spirit, his Holy Word, and godly and wise fellow pilgrims— overcome moral failure. You can pick up the fragmented pieces of your broken life and place them in the hands of the master potter. The end product will not be the same as it was before moral failure, but the restored soul will be different from, and in many ways much better than, before. There will always be scars that will remind you of where you have been. But as the potter in Jeremiah 18 formed again the vessel that was marred in his hands, so God, will make another pot, shaping it as seems best to him! Let God have his way. If God has his way, you will be blessed beyond your imagination. The end will be better than the beginning.

Conclusion

THERE IS INDEED A ROAD back to solid ground from the swamp of bad choices and bad behavior. While it may seem to be very difficult, the rewards of overcoming are overwhelmingly worth it. You will understand yourself and those around you in a way that you never thought possible. If you allow God to be in charge of your recovery, you will learn about his abounding grace in a way that you never could have otherwise. Take the prodigal son in Luke 15, who learned far more about his father's heart of forgiveness than his self-righteous older brother could ever have imagined. It is God's delight to show mercy, and that is just what we ragamuffins need more than anything.

I can't leave without saying something more about forgiveness. When God forgives us, he wipes the slate clean. "God is light … if we walk in the light, as he is in the light, we have fellowship with one another, and the blood of Jesus, his Son, purifies us from all sin … If we confess our sins, he is faithful and just and will forgive our sins and purify us from all unrighteousness" (1 John 1:5–9). We may or may not receive forgiveness from all those humans we have wronged. That will depend on them if we have done all that we can do. There is, however, a forgiveness that may be very slow in coming, and that is self-forgiveness. We tend to beat up on ourselves as a sort of penance or as a result of feelings of extreme guilt. What we need to realize is that if God can and does forgive us, then we ought to line up our thoughts with his. If the Supreme Being, the eternal God, says I am forgiven, then just as I had to align my thoughts with his about my sin, so I must align my thoughts with his about my forgiveness. "But, now a righteousness from God, apart from law, has been made known, … This righteousness from God comes through faith in Jesus Christ to all who believe. There is no difference, for all have sinned and fall short of the glory of God, and are justified freely by his grace through the redemption that came by Christ Jesus" (Romans 3:21–24).

Most of all, it is so wonderful to discover that "the truth will make you free!" The freedom that comes with the release from the bondage of moral failure and the realization that you don't have to be enslaved by your sin is like being granted a new lease on life. And that is literally what it is: a new life in which you can be free—really free!

> This is the word that came to Jeremiah from the Lord: 'Go down to the potter's house, and there I will give you my message.' So I went down to the potter's house, and I saw him working at the wheel. But the pot he was shaping from the clay was marred

in his hands; so the potter formed it into another pot, shaping it as seemed best to him. (Jeremiah 18: 1–4)

Therefore, prepare your minds for action; be self-controlled; set your hope fully on the grace to be given you when Jesus Christ is revealed. As obedient children, do not conform to the evil desires you had when you lived in ignorance. But just as he who called you is holy, so be holy in all you do; for it is written: 'Be holy, because I am holy.' Since you call on a Father who judges each man's work impartially, live your lives as strangers here in reverent fear. For you know that it was not with perishable things such as silver or gold that you were redeemed from the empty way of life handed down to you from your forefathers, but with the precious blood of Christ, a lamb without blemish or defect. He was chosen before the creation of the world, but was revealed in these last times for your sake. Through him you believe in God, who raised him from the dead and glorified him, and so your faith and hope are in God. (1 Peter 1:13–21)

No, in all these things we are more than conquerors through him who loved us. (Romans 8:37)

Humble yourselves before the Lord, and he will lift you up. (James 4:10)

So now the choice is yours. Choose life, truth, and freedom instead of death, deceit, and bondage. God is ready and willing to help if you are willing to "stop lying, especially to yourself" and to "be willing to do whatever takes." You can overcome moral failure!

CPSIA information can be obtained at www.ICGtesting.com
Printed in the USA
BVOW03s0325150114

341830BV00001B/4/P